BEST OF METALLICA

Front cover photo by James R. Minchin III

ISBN 1-57560-486-8

Visit our website at **www.cherrylane.com** 

Battery

Words and Music by James Hetfield and Lars Ulrich

E5
Fmaj7
F♯m7
G5
E5
Fmaj7
Vocal
Guitar I
Guitar II
Bass
Drums
F♯m7
G5
E5
Fmaj7
F♯m7
G5

Intro. 2
E5
Fmaj7
F♯m7
G5
F5
D(onF♯)
Vocal
Guitar I
Guitar II
Bass
Drums
H
P
3
M

E5
F5
D(onF♯)
G5
Vocal
Guitar I
Guitar II
Bass
Drums
Intro. 3
Tempo change
B5
B(onD♯)
B♭5
A5
M

E5
Em
B(onD♯) Em
E5
B♭5
A5
E5
F♯5
G5
E5
G5
G♯5
Vocal
Guitar I
Guitar II
Bass
Drums
M
T
A
B
E5
B♭5
A5
E5
Em
B(onD♯) Em
E5
B♭5
A5
B♭5 A5

Intro. 4
E5 B♭5 A5 E5 Em B(onD♯) Em E5 B♭5 A5 E5 F♯5 G5 E5 G5 G♯5
Vocal
Guitar I
Guitar II
Bass
Drums
E5 B♭5 A5 E5 Em B(onD♯) Em E5 B♭5 A5 B♭5 A5

E5
G5
A5
F5
B(onD♯)
Vocal
Guitar I
Guitar II
Bass
Drums
A
E5
B♭5
A5
E5
Em
B(onD♯) Em
E5
B♭5
A5
1. Lash - ing out the ac - tion, re - turn - ing the re - ac - tion, weak are ripped and torn a -
2. Crush - ing all de - ceiv - ers, mash - ing non - be - liev - ers, nev - er end - ing po - ten -
2x

E5 F♯5 G5 E5 G5 G♯5 E5 B♭5 A5 E5 Em B(onD♯)
Vocal
- way.
- cy.
Hyp - no - tiz - ing pow - er,
Hun - gry vi' - lence seek - er,
crush - ing all that cow - er,
feed - ing off the weak - er,
Guitar I
Guitar II
Bass
Drums
2x
Em E5 B♭5 A5 E5 F♯5 G5 E5 G5 G♯5 B E5
bat - ter - y is here to stay!
breed - ing on in - san - i - ty!
1., 2. Smash - ing through the bound - 'ries,

G5
A5
F5
B(onD♯)
E5
B♭5
A5
Vocal
lu - na - cy has found me,
can - not stop the bat - ter - y.
Guitar I
Guitar II
Bass
Drums
M
2x
E5
Em
B(onD♯) Em
E5
B♭5
A5
E5
F♯5
G5
E5
G5
G♯5

E5
G5
A5
F5
B(onD♯)
E5
B♭5
A5
Vocal
Pound-ing out ag-gres-sion turns in-to ob-ses-sion, can-not kill the bat-ter-y!
Guitar I
M
Guitar II
Bass
Drums
E5
Em
B(onD♯)
E5
B5
G5
Em
B(onD♯)
Can-not kill the fam-'ly, bat-ter-y has ground-ed
2x

E5 B♭5 A5 E5 Em B(onD♯) Em E5 B♭5 A5 B♭5 F5
Vocal
me!
Bat - ter -
Guitar I
Guitar II
Bass
Drums
2x
E5 B♭5 A5 E5 Em B(onD♯) Em E5 B♭5 A5
- y!

1.
B♭5
F5
E5
C
E5
G5
Vocal
Bat - ter - y!
Guitar I
Guitar II
Bass
Drums
A5
F5
B(onD♯)
2.
B♭5
F5
E5
Bat - ter - y!

D
E5
G5
Vocal
Guitar I
Guitar II
Bass
Drums
M
E5
G5
B5

E
E5
C5
D5
G5
A5
B5
Vocal
Guitar I
Guitar II
Bass
Drums
E5
C5
D5
G5
A5
B5
Vocal
Guitar I
Guitar II
Bass
Drums

E5
C5
D5
G5
A5
B5
Vocal
Guitar I
Guitar II
Bass
Drums
E5
G5
B5
G5
M
S

B♭5 A5
F E5 B♭5 A5 E5 B♭5 A5 E5 B♭5 A5
Vocal
Guitar I
Guitar II
Bass
Drums
E5 B♭5 A5 E5 B♭5 A5 E5 G5 F5 E5 B♭5 A5
8va
1H.C

Vocal
Guitar I
Guitar II
Bass
Drums
E
B♭5
A5
E5
1H.C
D
P
g
H
(8va)
M
6
3

Vocal
Guitar I
Guitar II
Bass
Drums
E5 B♭5 A5 E5 B♭5 A5 E5 G5 F5
E5 B♭5 A5 E B♭5 A5 E5 B♭5 A5 E5 B♭5 A5 B♭5 A5

G
E5
G5
A5
F♯5
Vocal
Guitar I
Guitar II
Bass
Drums
8va

H
F5 B♭5 B5 B♭5 B5 B♭5 B5 F♯5 F5 B♭5 B5 B♭5 B5 B♭5 B5 F♯5
Vocal
Guitar I
Guitar II
Bass
Drums
F5 B♭5 B5 B♭5 B5 B♭5 B5 F♯5 F5 B♭5 B5 B♭5 B5 B♭5 B5 F♯5
Vocal
Guitar I
Guitar II
Bass
Drums

F5
B(onD♯)
I
E5
B♭5
A5
3. Circle of destruction,
E5
Em
D(onF♯)
Em
E5
B♭5
A5
E5
F♯5
G5
E5
G5
G♯5
hammer comes crushing, power house of energy.
Vocal
Guitar I
Guitar II
Bass
Drums
M

E5 B♭5 A5 E5 Em B(onD♯) Em E5 B♭5 A5 E5 F♯5 G5 E5 G5 G♯5
Whip-ping up a fu - ry, dom-i-nat-ing flur - ry, we cre-ate the bat - ter - y!
Vocal
Guitar I
Guitar II
Bass
Drums
J
E5 G5 A5 F5 B(onD♯) E5 B♭5 A5
Smash-ing through the bound - 'ries, lu-na-cy has found me, can-not stop the bat - ter - y!
M

E5 Em B(onD♯) Em E5 B♭5 A5 E5 F♯5 G5 E5 G5 G♯5 E5
Vocal
Poung-ing out ag-gres-sion
Guitar I
Guitar II
Bass
Drums
G5 A5 F5 B(onD♯) E5 B♭5 A5 E5 Em B(onD♯)
turns in to ob-ses-sion, can-not kill the bat-ter-y!

E5 B5 G5 Em B(onD♯) E5 B♭5 A5 E5 Em B(onD♯)
Vocal
Can - not kill the fam - 'ly, bat - ter - y has ground - ed me!
Guitar I
M
Guitar II
Bass
Drums
Em E5 B♭5 A5 B♭5 F5 E5 B♭5 A5 E5 Em B(onD♯)
Bat - ter - y!

Em E5 B♭5 A5 B♭5 F5 E5 B♭5 A5 E5 Em B(onD♯)
Vocal
Bat - ter - y!
Guitar I
Guitar II
Bass
Drums
M
T A B
Em E5 B♭5 A5 B♭5 F5 E5 B♭5 A5 E5 Em B(onD♯)
Bat - ter - y!

Em E5
B♭5
A5
B♭5
F5
E5
K
F5
B♭5
B5
B♭5
B5
B♭5
B5
F♯5
Vocal
Bat - ter - y!
Guitar I
Guitar II
Bass
Drums
F5
B♭5
B5
B♭5
B5
B♭5
B5
F♯5
F5
B♭5
B5
B♭5
B5
B♭5
B5
F♯5

F5 B♭5 B5 B♭5 B5 B♭5 B5 F♯5 L F5 B♭5 B5 B♭5
Vocal
Guitar I
Guitar II
Bass
Drums
B5 B♭5 B5 F♯5 F5 B♭5 B5 B♭5 B5 B♭5 B5 F♯5

F5
B♭5
B5
B♭5
B5
B♭5
B5
F♯5
F5
B♭5
B5
B♭5
Vocal
Guitar I
Guitar II
Bass
Drums
B5
F♯5 F5
E5

Blackened

Words and Music by James Hetfield, Lars Ulrich and Jason Newsted

B
C
D
Em
Vocal
Guitar I
Guitar II
Bass
Drums
Tempo change
Intro.2
N.C.
E5

E5
Vocal
Guitar I
Guitar II
Bass
Drums
E5
G5
F♯5

Intro.3
G♯5
F♯5
E5
Vocal
Guitar I
Guitar II
Bass
Drums
M
T
A
B
E5

E5
Intro.4
E5
Vocal
Guitar I
Guitar II
Bass
Drums
M
M
E5
Vocal
Guitar I
Guitar II
Bass
Drums

A
E5
Vocal
Black-ened is the end.
Blis-ter-ing of Earth.
Win-ter it will send.
Ter-min-ate its worth.
Throw-ing all you see in-
Dead-ly nic-o-tine,
Guitar I
M
Guitar II
Bass
Drums
G5
- to ob-scur-i-ty.
kills what might have been.
E5
Death of Moth-er Earth.
Cal-lous frig-id chill.
Nev-er a re-birth.
Noth-ing left to kill.
2x

E5
G5
Vocal
Ev - o - lu - tion's end.
Nev - er seen be - fore.
Nev - er will it mend.
Breath - ing nev - er more.
Guitar I
Guitar II
Bass
Drums
2x
B
Nev - er.

E5
C
E5
A5
Vocal
Fire.
To be -
Guitar I
Guitar II
Bass
Drums
D5
G5
C5
G5
F♯5
G5
F♯5
- gin whip - ping dance of the dead.
Black - ened is the

E5 A5 D5 G5 C5 G5 F♯5
Vocal
end. To be - gin whip - ping dance of the dead.
Guitar I
Guitar II
Bass
Drums
G5 F♯5 D E5
1.
Col-or our world black-ened.

2.
Tempo change
G5
F♯5
F5
E5
E♭5
Vocal
Black - ened.
Guitar I
Guitar II
Bass
Drums

E5
E♭5
E5
Vocal
Guitar I
M
g
Guitar II
Bass
Drums
E5
E♭5
E5
Vocal
Guitar I
Guitar II
Bass
Drums

E5
Vocal
Guitar I
Guitar II
Bass
Drums
E♭5
E5
F
E5
Op - pos - i - tion.
Con - tra - dic - tion,
Op - pos - i - tion.
Con - tra - dic - tion,
Prem - o -

E5
Prem - o - ni - tion.
E♭5
E5
Ag - i - na - tion.
Vocal
- ni - tion.
Com - pro - mise.
Ag - i - ta - tion.
Vi - o -
Guitar I
M
g
Guitar II
Bass
Drums
E5
Vi - o - la - tion.
Mu - ti - la - tion.
E♭5
- la - tion.
Mu - ti - la - tion.
Plan - et dies.
4

G
F♯5
F5
Vocal
Dark - est col - or.
Blis - tered earth.
True death of life.
Guitar I
Guitar II
Bass
Drums
H
E5
E♭5
E5

E5
Vocal
Guitar I
Guitar II
Bass
Drums
E♭5
I E5
Ter - mi - na - tion. Ex - pi - ra - tion. Can - cel -
Ter - mi - na - tion. Ter - mi - na - tion. Ex - pi - ra - tion.

E5
- a - tion.
E♭5
Ex - pec - ta - tion.
E5
Lib - er - a - tion.
Pop - u -
Vocal
Can - cel - a - tion hu - man race.
Ex - pec - ta - tion.
Lib - er - a - tion.
Guitar I
Guitar II
Bass
Drums
E5
- la - tion.
E♭5
J F♯5
Pop - u - la - tion lay to waste.
See our moth - er put to death.

F♯5
F5
K E5
D5
C5
Vocal
See our moth - er die.
Guitar I
Guitar II
Bass
Drums
C5 B5 G5 F♯5
E5
D5
C5
B5
G5 F♯5

E5
D5
C5
B5
G5
F♯5
Vocal
Guitar I
Guitar II
Bass
Drums
H P

E5 D5 C5 B5 G5 F♯5 E5 D5 C5 B5 G5 F♯5
Vocal
Guitar I
Guitar II
Bass
Drums
L E5
M

E5
Vocal
Guitar I
Guitar II
Bass
Drums
E5
8va

E5
Vocal
with Harmonizer
Guitar I
Guitar II
Bass
Drums
E5
(with Hamonizer)
(8va)

Tempo change
N.C.
M
G5
F♯5
G5
F♯5
F5
Vocal
Guitar I
Guitar II
Bass
Drums
N
E5
8va
C
g

E5
Vocal
Guitar I
Guitar II
Bass
Drums
(8va)
Arm

O
E5
A5
D5
G5
C5
G5
F#5
Vocal
Guitar I
Guitar II
Bass
Drums
H
P
M
g
G5
F#5
E5
A5
D5
G5
C5
G5

F#5
G5
P
E5
Vocal
Guitar I
Harm. , 8va
Harm.
Arm
Guitar II
M
Bass
Drums
A5
G5
C5
G5

E5
A5
G5
Vocal
Guitar I
Harm.
Arm
Guitar II
Bass
Drums
C5
G5
Q
E5
(Harm.)
(Arm)
(M)

E5
Vocal
Guitar I
Guitar II
Bass
Drums
M
T
A
B
4
6
4

R
E5
Vocal
Smoul-der-ing de-cay.
Take her breath a-way.
Mil-lions of our years in
Guitar I
Guitar II
Bass
Drums
G5
min-utes dis-ap-pears.
E5
Dark-en-ing in vain.
Dec-a-dence re-mains.

E5
G5
S
E5
Vocal
All is said and done.
Nev - er is the sun.
Nev - er.
Guitar I
Guitar II
Bass
Drums
E5
Vocal
Guitar I
Guitar II
Bass
Drums

T
E5
A5
D5
G5
C5
G5
F♯5
Vocal
Fire. To be - gin whip - ping dance of the dead.
Fire. is the out - come of hy - poc - ri - cy.
Guitar I
Guitar II
Bass
Drums
G5
F♯5
E5
A5
D5
G5
C5
G5
Black - ened is the end. To be - gin whip - ping dance of the
Dark - est po - ten - cy. In the ex - it of hu - man - i -
2x

1.
2.
F♯5
G5
F♯5
G5
F♯5
Vocal
dead.
- ty.
Col - or our world black - ened.
Guitar I
Guitar II
M
M→
Bass
Drums
G5
F♯5
F5
E5
Black - ened.
(M)
M
M
M
M

Enter Sandman

Words and Music by James Hetfield, Lars Ulrich and Kirk Hammett

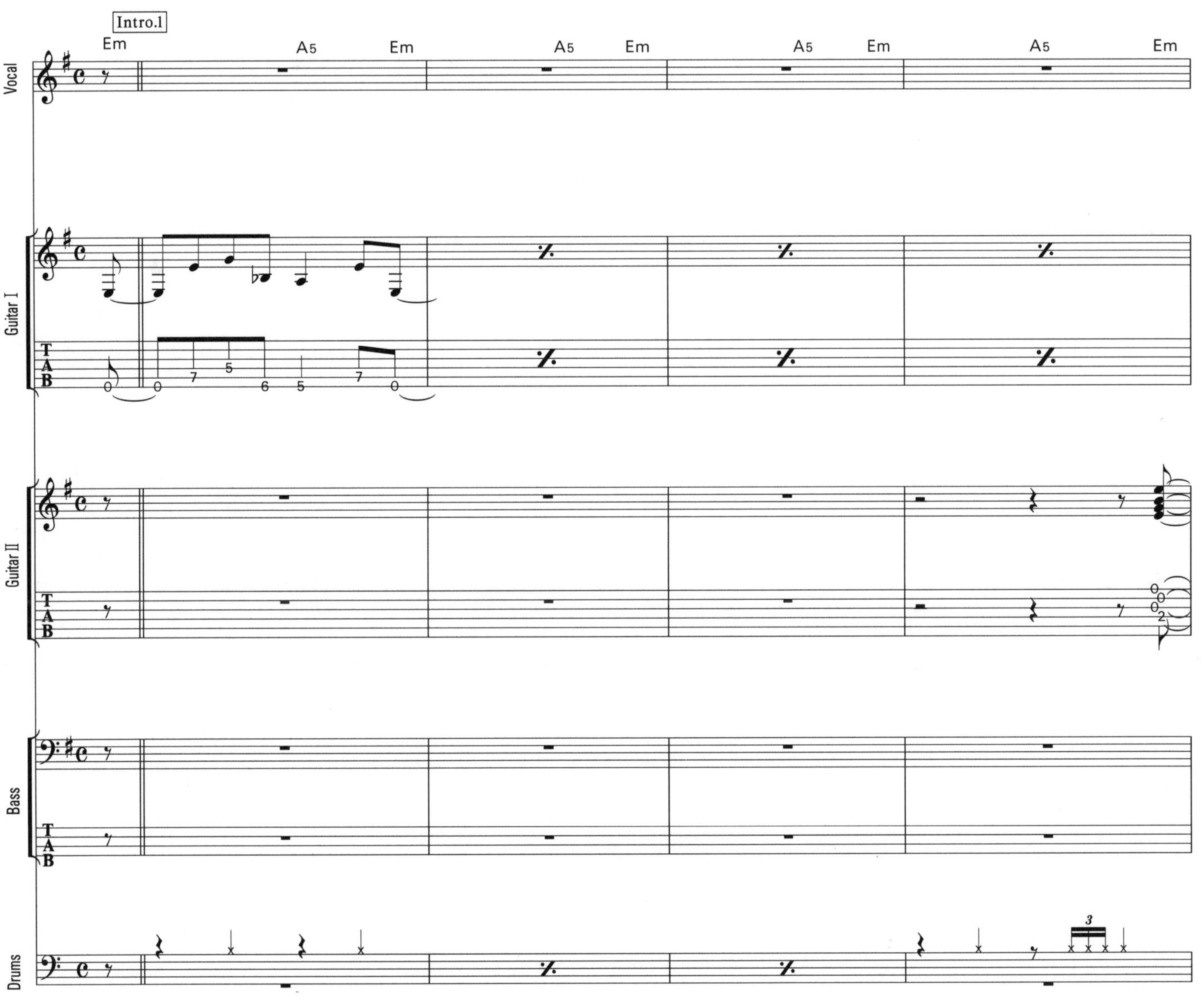

Vocal
Guitar I
Guitar II
Bass
Drums
Em
A5
Intro.2

Intro.3
E5
Vocal
Guitar I
M
Guitar II
Bass
Drums
Intro.4
E5
F5
E5
F5
E5
F5
E5
A5
E5
Vocal
Guitar I
M
Guitar II
Bass
Drums

E5
A5
F5
Vocal
Guitar I
Guitar II
Bass
Drums
M
g
T
A
B
E5
A5
F5
E5
A5
E5

Intro.5
E5 A5 E5 A5 E5 A5 E5 F#5 G5 F#5 E5
Vocal
Guitar I
Guitar II
Bass
Drums
A
E5 F5 E5 F5 E5 G5
1. Say your prayers, lit - tle one. Don't for - get my son, to in - clude ev - 'ry - one.
2. Some - thing's wrong. shut the light. Heav - y thoughts to - night, and they aren't of Snow White.

G5
F♯5
G5
F♯5
G5
F5
E5
F5
Vocal
I tuck you in, warm with - in, keep you free from sin
Dreams of war, dreams of liars, dreams of dra - gon's fire
Guitar I
M
Guitar II
2x Another Gt.
g
Bass
Drums
4
E5
G5
F♯5
G5
F♯5
F♯m
B
B5
F♯m
B5
F♯m
till the sand - man he comes.
and of things that will bite.
Sleep with one eye o - pen,

F♯m
B5
F♯m
B5
C
F♯5
B5
F♯5
B5
F♯5
Vocal
grip - ping your pil - low tight.
Ex - it: light.
Guitar I
Guitar II
Bass
Drums
F♯5
B5
E5
F♯5
B5
E5
En - ter: night.
Take my hand.
2x
S

E5
1.
G5 F♯5 G5 F♯5 E5
D
A5 E5
A5 E5
Vocal
We're off to nev - er nev - er land.
Guitar I
Guitar II
Bass
Drums
M
E5 A5 G5
F♯5 G5 F♯5 E5
A5 G5
A5 E5
Another Gt.

E5 A5 G5 F♯5 G5 F♯5 E5
2.
G5 F♯5 G5 F♯5 E5
off to nev - er nev - er land.
Heh, heh
E
E5 A5 E5 A5 E5
Vocal
Guitar I
Guitar II
Bass
Drums
Port.C
Q.C

Vocal
Guitar I
Guitar II
Bass
Drums
E5
A5
G5
F♯5
F♯m

F
F♯m
B5
C
S
P
M
Vocal
Guitar I
Guitar II
Bass
Drums
F♯5
E5
Arm

Vocal
Guitar I
Guitar II
Bass
Drums
F♯5
B5
E5
8va
Arm
G
F5

H
Em
A5
Now I lay me down to sleep.
(Now I lay me down to sleep.)
Pray the Lord my soul to keep.
(Pray the Lord my soul to keep.)
If I die before I wake,
(If I die before I wake,)
Pray the Lord my soul to take.
(Pray the Lord my soul to take.)
F♯m
Vocal
Guitar I
Guitar II
Bass
Drums
(Arm)

I
F♯m
B5
Vocal
Hush, lit - tle ba - by. don't stay a word.
And nev - er mind that noise you heard.
Guitar I
Guitar II
M
Bass
Drums
It's just the beasts un - der your bed.
In your clo - set, in your head.
g

J
F♯5 B5 F♯5 B5 F♯5 B5 E5
Vocal
Ex - it: light.
En - ter: night.
Guitar I
Guitar II
M
Bass
Drums
F♯5 B5 E5 F♯5 B5 F♯5 B5 F♯5
Grain of sand.
Ex - it: light.

F♯5 B5 E5 F♯5 B5 E5
Vocal
En - ter: night. Take my hand. We're
Guitar I
Guitar II
M
Bass
S
Drums
G5 F♯5 G5 F♯5 E5
K
E5 A5 E5 A5 E5
off to nev - er nev - er land. Yeah. Ha ha ha ha ha ha. Oo!
T
A
B

E5 A5 E5 A5 E5 A5 E5 A5 E5
Vocal
Yeah, yeah!
Guitar I
Guitar II
Bass
Drums
E5 A5 G5 F♯5 G5 F♯5 Em L A5 Em A5 Em
Yo, woh!
M

Em
A5
Em
A5
Em
A5
Em
A5
Em
A5
Em
Vocal
Ex - it: take my hand.
(We're off to never never land.)
Guitar I
Guitar II
Bass
Drums
Em
A5
Em
A5
Em
A5
Em
A5
Em
Ex - it: take my hand.
(We off to never never land.)
M
M
0 0 7 0 0 0 0 0
0 0 0 0 0 0 0 0

Vocal
Guitar I
Guitar II
Bass
Drums
Em
A5
(We off to never never land.)
Another Gt.
H P
(We off to never never land.)

Em
A5
Em
A5
Em
A5
Em
Vocal
(We off to never never land.)
Guitar I
Guitar II
S S
P
g
S
Bass
Drums
Fade Out

Fight Fire With Fire

Words and Music by James Hetfield, Lars Ulrich and Cliff Burton

G
Am
G(onB)
C
Am
G(onB)
Bm7
A
Vocal
Guitar I
Guitar II
Bass
Drums
H P
S
P
G
Am
G(onB)
C
Am
G(onB)
A
G
Vocal
Guitar I
Guitar II
Bass
Drums

G
Am
G(onB)
C
Am
G(onB)
Em
G5
C
Vocal
Guitar I
Guitar II
Bass
Drums
H P
S
Intro.2
Tempo Change
C
E5
G5
E5
F♯5
E5
G5
E5
F♯5
E5
F♯5
M

E5 G5 E5 F♯5 E5 G5 E5 F♯5 E5 F5 E5 G5 E5 F♯5
Vocal
Guitar I
Guitar II
Bass
Drums
E5 G5 E5 F♯5 E5 F♯5 E5 G5 E5 F♯5 E5 G5 E5 F♯5 E5 F5

E5
G5
E5
F#5
E5
G5
E5
F#5
E5
F#5
E5
G5
E5
F#5
Vocal
Guitar I
Guitar II
Bass
Drums
E5
G5
E5
F#5
E5
F5
E5
G5
E5
F#5
E5
G5
E5
F#5
E5
F#5

Intro.3
E5 G5 E5 F#5 E5 G5 E5 F#5 E5 F5 E5 F#5 G5
Vocal
Guitar I
Guitar II
Bass
Drums
E5 F#5 E5 F#5 G5 E5 F#5

E5 F♯5 G5 E5 F♯5 E5 F♯5 G5
Vocal
Guitar I
Guitar II
Bass
Drums
E5 F♯5
A
E5 G5 E5 F♯5 E5 G5 E5 F♯5 G5 F♯5
1. Do un - to oth - ers
2. Blow the u - ni - verse

E5 G5 E5 F♯5 E5 G5 E5 F♯5 E5 F5 E5 G5 E5 F♯5
as they've done to you. But what
in - to noth - ing - ness. Nu - cle -
Vocal
Guitar I
Guitar II
Bass
Drums
E5 G5 E5 F♯5 E5 F♯5 E5 G5 E5 F♯5 E5 G5 E5 F♯5 E5 F5
- the hell is this world com - ing to?
- ar war - fare shall lay us to rest.
2x

B
E5
F♯5
G5
Vocal
Guitar I
Guitar II
Bass
Drums
P
1.
2.
C
B♭5
B5
Fight fi - re with fi - re.
M

B♭5
E5 G5 E5 B♭5 B5 B♭5
Vocal
End - ing is near.
Guitar I
Guitar II
Bass
Drums
E5 G5 E5 B♭5 B5 B♭5
E5 G5 E5 B♭5 B5 B♭5
Fight fi - re with fi - re.
Burst - ing with fear.

B♭5
D
E5
G5
E5
F♯5
We all shall die!
F5

E5 G5 E5 F♯5 E5 F♯5 E5 G5 E5 F♯5 E5 G5 E5 F♯5 E5 F5
Vocal
Guitar I
Guitar II
Bass
Drums
E
E5 G5 E5 F♯5 E5 G5 E5 F♯5 E5 F♯5 E5 G5 E5 F♯5
3. Time is like a fuse, short and
M

E5 G5 E5 F#5 E5 F5 E5 G5 E5 F#5 E5 F#5 E5 G5 E5 F#5 E5 F#5
Vocal
burn - ing fast. Ar - ma - ged - don's here,
Guitar I
Guitar II
Bass
Drums
E5 G5 E5 F#5 E5 G5 E5 F#5 E5 F5 F E5 F#5 G5
like said in the past.
Guitar I
Guitar I
Bass
Drums

E5
F♯5
E5
F♯5
G5
E5
F♯5
Vocal
Guitar I
Guitar II
Bass
Drums
G
E5
G5
E5
B♭5
B5
B♭5
Fight fi - re with fi - re.
End - ing is near.
M

B♭5
E5 G5 E5 B♭5 B5 B♭5
Vocal
Fight fi - re with fi - re.
Guitar I
Guitar II
Bass
Drums
E5 G5 E5 B♭5 B5 B♭5
D5 C5 B5
H
A5
Burst - ing with fear.
M

A5
G5
A5
B5
C5
B5
G5
A5
Vocal
Guitar I
Guitar I
Bass
Drums
M
S
H
I
E5
Guitar II
H.U
U
C
D
P

E5
A5
G5
Vocal
Guitar I
Guitar II
Bass
Drums
F♯5
E5

E5
A5
Vocal
Guitar I
Guitar II
Bass
Drums
G5
F♯5
J
E5 F♯5 G5 E5 F♯5 G5

E5 F♯5 G5 E5 F♯5 G5
E5 F♯5 G5 E5 F♯5 G5
E5 F♯5 G5 E5 F♯5 G5
Vocal
Guitar I
Guitar II
Bass
Drums
8va
K
E5
M
2x

E5
A5
Vocal
Guitar I
Guitar II
Bass
Drums
G5
1.
2.
F♯5
F♯5
(8va)

L
E5 F♯5 G5 E5 F♯5 G5 E5 F♯5 G5 E5 F♯5 G5
E5 F♯5 G5 E5 F♯5 G5 E5 F♯5 G5 E5 F♯5 G5
Vocal
Guitar I
Guitar II
Bass
Drums
E5

M
E5 G5 E5 F♯5 E5 G5 E5 F♯5 E5 F♯5 E5 G5 E5 F♯5
Vocal
Guitar I
Guitar II
Bass
Drums
E5 G5 E5 F♯5 E5 F5 E5 G5 E5 F♯5 E5 G5 E5 F♯5 E5 F♯5
Vocal
Guitar I
Guitar II
Bass
Drums

E5 G5 E5 F♯5 E5 G5 E5 F♯5 E5 F5
N
Vocal
Guitar I
Guitar II
Bass
Drums
4. Soon to
fill our lungs, the hot winds of death.

E5
G5
F#5
F5
O
Vocal
The gods are laugh - ing, so take your last breath.
Guitar I
Guitar II
Bass
Drums
T
A
B
P

E5
F♯5
G5
E5
F♯5
P
F5
G5
E5
B♭5
B5
B♭5
Vocal
Fight fi - re with fi - re.
Guitar I
Guitar II
Bass
Drums
B♭5
E5
G5
E5
B♭5
B5
B♭5
End - ing is near.

E5 G5 E5 B♭5 B5 B♭5
Vocal
Fight fi - re with fi - re.
E5 G5 E5 B♭5 B5 B♭5
Burst - ing with fear.
Guitar I
Guitar II
Bass
Drums
Q
E5 G5 E5 B♭5 B5 B♭5
Fight fi - re with fi - re. Fight fi - re with fi - re. Fight fi - re with fi - re. Fight fi - re with fi - re.
M

E5 G5 E5 B♭5 B5 B♭5 E5 G5 E5 B♭5 B5 B♭5 E5 G5 E5 B♭5 B5 B♭5 E5 G5 E5 B♭5 B5 B♭5
Vocal
Fight fi - re with fi - re. Fight fi - re with fi - re. Fight fi - re with fi - re. Fight fi - re with fi - re.
Guitar I
Guitar II
Bass
Drums
R
E5 G5 E5 B♭5 B5 B♭5 E5 G5 E5 B♭5 B5 B♭5 E5 G5 E5 B♭5 B5 B♭5 E5 G5 E5 B♭5 B5 B♭5
Vocal
Fight!
Guitar I
Guitar II
Bass
Drums

E5 G5 E5 B♭5 B5 B♭5
Vocal
Guitar I
Guitar II
Bass
Drums
B♭5
E5
Harm.
Arm.
g

For Whom the Bell Tolls

Words and Music by James Hetfield, Lars Ulrich and Cliff Burton

Intro.2
E5
F♯5
E5
Vocal
Other
Guitar I
Guitar II
( ) = Another Bass
8va
Bass
Drums
Intro.3
E5
F♯5
E5
F♯5
2x

1.
2.
E5
F♯5
Vocal
Other
Guitar I
Guitar II
Bass
Drums
Intro.4
2x

E5
F#5
Intro.5
N.C.
Vocal
Other
Guitar I
Guitar II
Bass
Drums
M
(M)
2x
N.C.

Intro.6
E5
G5
Vocal
Other
Guitar I
Guitar II
Bass
Drums
2x

1.
2.
E5
G5
C5
A5
Vocal
Other
Guitar I
Guitar II
Bass
Drums
Intro.7
B♭5
F♯5
(M)
M

E5
G5
E5
B♭5
F♯5
F5
A
E5
1. Make his fight on the hill in the ear - ly day.
2. Take a look to the sky just be fore you die.
G5
Con - stant chill deep in - side.
It's the last time he will.
E5
Shout - ing gun, on they
Black - ened roar, mas - sive
Vocal
Other
Guitar I
Guitar II
Bass
Drums
M
2x

E5
G5
C5
A5
Vocal
run through the end - less grey.
roar fills the crum - bling sky.
On they fight, for they're right.
Shat - tered goal fills his soul
Yes, but who's to say?
with a ruth - less cry.
Other
Guitar I
Guitar II
Bass
Drums
2x
E5
G5
For a hill men would kill. Why? They do not know.
Stran - ger now are his eyes to this mys - ter - y.
Suf - fered wounds test their
Hears the si - lence so

G5
E5
Vocal
pride.
loud.
Men of five, still a - live through the rag - ing glow.
Crack of dawn, all is gone ex - pect the will to be.
Other
Guitar I
Guitar II
Bass
Drums
2x
G5
C5
A5
B
E5
G5
E5
A5
Gone in - sane from the pain that they sure - ly know.
Now they see what will be, blind - ed eyes to see.
M

E5 G5 B♭5 F♯5 E5 G5 E5 A5 E5 G5 E5 B♭5 F♯5 F5
Vocal
For whom the bell tolls.
For whom the bell tolls.
Time march - es
Time march - es
Other
Guitar I
Guitar II
Bass
Drums
M
E5 G5 E5 A5 E5 G5 B♭5 F♯5 E5 G5 E5 A5
1.
E5 G5 E5 B♭5 F♯5 F5
on
on
for whom the bell tolls.
for whom the bell tolls.

C
E5
G5
Vocal
Other
Guitar I
Guitar II
Bass
Drums
M
E5
B5
E5
( ) = Another Gt.

E5
G5
Vocal
Other
Guitar I
Guitar II
Bass
Drums
E5
B5
2.
E5
G5 E5
B♭5
F♯5
F5

D
E5
F♯5
G5
Vocal
Other
Guitar I
Guitar II
Bass
Drums
Harm.
Arm
(Harm.)

G5
E5
F#5
Vocal
Other
Guitar I
Harm.
Arm
C
H
8va
Guitar II
Bass
Drums

E5 F♯5 G5 E5 F♯5 E5 F♯5
Vocal
Other
Guitar I
Arm Arm
Arm H P H P H P H Arm
Arm H Arm
Guitar II
Bass
Drums
G5 E5 F♯5 E5 F♯5 G5
Arm
Arm H P
Arm
Arm

Vocal
Other
Guitar I
Guitar II
Bass
Drums
E5
F♯5
G5
Arm
C
D
8va
(8va)
Fade Out

Fuel

Words and Music by James Hetfield, Lars Ulrich and Kirk Hammett

Intro.2
E5
Vocal
Guitar I
Guitar II
Bass
Drums
P
2x
1.
2.
Intro.3
G5 A5
G5
A5
Q.C
S
H

A5
E5
Vocal
Yeah.
Guitar I
Q.C
g
P
Guitar II
Bass
Drums
A
E5
G5
E5
1. Turn on, I see red.
3. Turn on be - yond the bone.
H
2x

E5
B5
B♭5
Vocal
A - dren - a - line crash and crack my head.
Swal - low fu - ture, spit out home,
Ni - tro junk - ie, paint
burn your face up - on
Guitar I
Guitar II
Q.C
Bass
Drums
2x
A5
B
A5
me dead.
the chrome.
And
H

A5
E5
Yeah.
oh yeah.
C E5
I see red.
2. A hun-dred plus through
4. Take the cor - ner,
Vocal
Guitar I
Guitar II
Bass
Drums
Q.C
P
g
H
S
2x
G5
E5
black and white,
join the crash,
ah.
ah.

E5
B5
B♭5
Vocal
War horse, war - head. Fuck 'em, man, white
Head - lights. Head - lines. An - oth - er junk - ie lives
Guitar I
Guitar II
Bass
Drums
2x
A5
D
- knuck - le tight
too fast,
through
Yeah,
Q.C
H
P
S
g

A5
E5
Vocal
black and white.
lives way too fast,
fast,
fast,
Guitar I
Q.C
g
P
Guitar II
Bass
Drums
Ooh,
on I burn.
woh.
E
Harm.
M
2x

A5
G6
A5
Vocal
Fuel is pump - ing en - gines,
burn - ing hard,
Guitar I
Guitar II
Bass
Drums
2x
A5
E5
Ooh,
A5
loose and clean.
And on I burn.

A5
C
Churn - ing my di - rec - tion,
quench my
D
E5
thirst with gas - o - line.
So gim - me
Vocal
Guitar I
Guitar II
Bass
Drums
2x
2x

F
E5
Vocal
fuel, gim - me fire, gim - me that which I de - sire.
1.
Guitar I
P P P
Guitar II
g
Bass
Drums
G
E5
Yeah.
G5 A5 G5 A5
S S S
P P P

E5
G5 A5
G5 A5
Vocal
Guitar I
Guitar II
Bass
Drums
H
A5
Q.C

E5
2.
N.C.
Ooh,
yeah.
Vocal
Guitar I
Guitar II
Bass
Drums
I
E5
1.
G5
M
2x

2.
E5
G5
J
E5
Vocal
Guitar I
Guitar II
Bass
Drums
M
g
1.
K
A5
H
2x, Another Gt.
C
2x

Vocal
Guitar I
Guitar II
Bass
Drums
A5
G5
E5
M
Port. H.C
H
g
C
H.C
D
1.
2x
4

2.
G5
L
A5
Vocal
Guitar I
Guitar II
Bass
Drums
H.C
Q.C
H
A5
M
E5
White - knuck - le tight.
C D P
g
P
8va

Vocal
Guitar I
Guitar II
Bass
Drums
E5
G5 A5 G5 A5
E5
E5
G5 A5 G5 A5
N
E5 G5
E5 G5
(8va)
8va

E5 G5 A5 G5 A5 E5 G5 E5 G5
Vocal
Guitar I
Guitar II
Bass
Drums
E5 G5 F♯5 F5 E5
Vocal
Guitar I
Guitar II
Bass
Drums

E5
G5
A5
G5
A5
O
E5
Vocal
Guitar I
Harm.
M
P
Guitar II
g
Another Gt.
Bass
S
H
Drums
E5
A5
Gim - me

Vocal
Guitar I
Guitar II
Bass
Drums
G6
A5
E5
fuel.
gim - me fi - re.

A5
C
D
Vocal
my de - si - re.
Guitar I
Guitar II
Bass
Drums

P
E5
A5
G6
Vocal
Guitar I
Guitar II
Bass
Drums
Ooh, on I born.
Fuel is pump - ing en - gines, burn - ing hard,

A5
E5
Ooh,
loose and clean.
And on and on.
Vocal
Guitar I
Guitar II
Bass
Drums
Another Gt.
Another Gt.
A5
C
Churn - ing my di - rec - tion,

Vocal
Guitar I
Guitar II
Bass
Drums
C
D
quench my thirst with gas - o - line.
E5
Q
Gim - me fuel, gim - me fire, gim - me that which I de - sire,

E5
G5 A5
G5
A5
Vocal
ooh!
Guitar I
Guitar II
Bass
Drums
R
A5
On
I
burn.
E5
Q.C
C
H
g

Master of Puppets

Words and Music by James Hetfield, Lars Ulrich, Kirk Hammett and Cliff Burton

D
D♭
C
Em
Em
Vocal
Guitar I
Guitar II
Bass
Drums
M
1.2.
3x

3.
Intro.3
Em
Em
Vocal
Guitar I
Guitar II
Bass
Drums
M
Intro.4
Em
Em
(M)
S

Em
B5
Em
Vocal
Guitar I
(M)
M
Guitar II
Bass
Drums
2x
Em
G5
S

Intro.5
G5
E5
Em
Em
Vocal
Guitar I
Guitar II
Bass
Drums

Em
Vocal
Guitar I
Guitar II
Bass
Drums
M
S
H
𝄋1.2. (with Repeat)
A
Em
1. End of pas - sion play,
crum - bl - ing a - way,
2. Nee - dle - work the way,
nev - er you be - tray,
3. Hell is worth all that,
nat - 'ral hab - i - tat,
3x

Em
I'm your source of self - de - struc - tion.
life of death be - com - ing clear - er.
just a rhyme with - out a rea - son.
Vocal
Guitar I
Guitar II
Bass
Drums
2,3x
Em
Veins that pump with fear,
Pain mo - nop - o - ly,
Nev - er - end - ing maze,
suck - ing dark - est clear,
rit - ual mis - er - y,
drift on num - bered days,

Em
Vocal
lead - ing on your death's con - struc - tion.
chop your break - fast on a mir - ror.
now your life is out of sea - son.
Guitar I
Guitar II
Bass
Drums
2,3x
B F♯m
1.2. Taste me you will see,
3. I will oc - cu - py,
more is all you need,
I will help you die,
M
M→
S
H
2x
3x

F♯m
Vocal
ded - i - cat - ed to
I will run through you,
how I'm kill - ing you.
now I rule you too.
Guitar I
Guitar II
Bass
Drums
F♯m
C
E5
D5
E5
B5
C5
B5
Come

C5
D♯5
B5
E5
D5
E5
B5
C5
B5
Vocal
crawl - ing
1. fast - er,
2. mas - ter,
3. fast - er,
o -
your
o -
Guitar I
Guitar II
Bass
Drums
1.2.
3.
N.C.
- bey your
life burns
- bey your
mas - ter,
2x

F
D
E5
G
C5
B5
A5
Vocal
Guitar I
Guitar II
Bass
Drums
mas - ter. Mas - ter of Pup - pets, I'm pull - ing your strings,
twist - ing your mind and smash - ing your dreams.
M
P
2x

A5
D
C5
Vocal
Blind - ed by me, you can't see a
Guitar I
Guitar II
Bass
Drums
2x
3x
B
E5
D5
C
thing, just call my name 'cause I'll hear you scream.

C
E5
F
E5
Vocal
Mas - ter,
mas - ter.
Just call my name, 'cause I'll
Guitar I
Guitar II
Bass
Drums
E5
C
hear you
scream.
2x
3x

to Φ 1.2.
E5
F
E
Em
Vocal
Mas - ter,
mas - ter.
Guitar I
M
Guitar II
Bass
Drums
Em
B5
Em
(M)

Em
G5
Vocal
Guitar I
Guitar II
Bass
Drums
D.S.1.
Coda 1.
F
N.C.
Tempo change
F
Em
D
C7
Mas - ter,
mas - ter,
mas - ter.
rit.

Vocal
Guitar I
Guitar II
Bass
Drums
C2
A2
B7
B7(onD♯)
Em
D
C2
G
8va

Vocal
Guitar I
Guitar II
Bass
Drums
D
C2
A2
B7
B7(onD♯)
Em
D
C2
A2
B7
B7(onD♯)

H
Em
D
C2
A2
B7
B7(onD♯)
Vocal
Guitar I
Guitar II
Bass
Drums

C2
A2
B7
B7(onD♯)
I
Em
D
Vocal
Guitar I
Guitar II
Bass
Drums
C2
A7
B7(onD♯)

J
Em
D
C2
A2
Vocal
Guitar I
Guitar II
Bass
Drums
2x
B7
B7(onD♯)
E5

K
F♯5 G5 F♯5 G5
Vocal
Guitar I
Guitar II
Bass
Drums
M
L
Mas - ter, mas - ter, where's the dreams that I've been af - ter? Mas - ter, mas - ter,

F♯5 G5 F♯5 G5 F♯5 G5 F♯5 G5 F♯5 G5 F♯5 G5
Vocal
promised only lies.__ Laughter, laughter, all I hear__ or see__ is laughter.
Guitar I
Guitar II
Bass
Drums
F♯5 G5 F♯5 G5 F♯5 G5 F♯5 G5
Tempo change
M G
Laughter, laughter, laughing at__ my cries.__

F♯
N Em
Vocal
Guitar I
Pick Scratch
g
8va
P
Guitar II
M
S
Bass
H
Drums
Em
5/8

Vocal
Guitar I
Guitar II
Bass
Drums
Em
Harm.
Arm
(8va)

Em
O
F♯m
Vocal
Guitar I
Guitar II
Bass
Drums
8va
H
S
M
F♯m
C
P
H.C

F♯m
Vocal
Guitar I
Guitar II
Bass
Drums
1.5C
B5
P
E5
F5
E5
F5
E5
F5
E5
F5
E5
B5
Arm
2x

Vocal
Guitar I
Guitar II
Bass
Drums
E5 F5 E5 F5 E5 F5 E5 F5 E5 B5 E5
Q
Em
C
Em
2x

R
Em
C
Em
C
Vocal
Guitar I
Guitar II
Bass
Drums
M
(M)

C
E5
C
Vocal
Guitar I
Guitar II
Bass
Drums
Em
G5
1.

2.
G5
Coda 2.
F
mas - ter,
D.S.2.
T
Em
Vocal
Guitar I
Guitar II
Bass
Drums

Em
Vocal
Guitar I
Guitar II
Bass
Drums
T
A
B
Em

Vocal
Guitar I
Guitar II
Bass
Drums
Em
8va
N.C.
G5
E5
Ha! Ha! Ha! Ha!

One

Words and Music by James Hetfield and Lars Ulrich

Intro.2
D(onA)
Gmaj7
N.C.
Bm
Gmaj7
Vocal
Guitar I
Guitar II
Bass
Drums
Bm
Gmaj7
Bm
D(onA)

Intro.3
Gmaj7
N.C.
Bm
Gmaj7
Vocal
Guitar I
Guitar II
Bass
Drums
8va
Bm
Gmaj7
Bm
D(onA)

Intro.4
Gmaj7
B5
Bm
Gmaj7
Vocal
Guitar I
Guitar II
Bass
Drums
H
S
Bm
Gmaj7
Bm
D(onA)

Intro.5
Gmaj7
Em
F♯m
G5
A5
D
G
F
Em
Vocal
Guitar I
Guitar II
Bass
Drums

D
G
F
Em
C5
A
Bm
Gmaj7
Bm
Vocal
Guitar I
Guitar II
Bass
Drums
1. I can't re - mem - ber an - y - thing, can't tell if this is
2. Back in the womb it's much too real, in pumps life that

Gmaj7
Bm
D(on A)
Vocal
true or dream. Deep down in-side I feel to scream,
I must feel, but can't look for-ward to re-veal,
Guitar I
Guitar II
Bass
Drums
2x
Gmaj7
N.C.
Bm
Gmaj7
this ter-ri-ble si-lence stops me. Now that the war is through with me,
look to the time when I'll live. Fed through the tube that sticks in me,

Bm
Gmaj7
Bm
Vocal
I'm wak - ing up, I can not see
just like a war - time nov - el - ty;
that there's not much
tied to ma - chines that
Guitar I
Guitar II
Bass
Drums
2x
D(onA)
Gmaj7
N.C.
B
G5
A5 B5 A5
left to me.
make me be.
Noth - ing is real but pain now!
Cut this life off from me!
Hold my breath as

G5
F♯5
B5
A5
B5
C♯5
B5
A5
C5
C♯5
C D
Vocal
I wish for death.
Oh please God, wake me!
Guitar I
Guitar II
Bass
Drums
G
F
1.
Em

D
G
F
Vocal
Guitar I
Guitar II
Bass
Drums
Em
2.
Em
D
D

G
F
Em
Vocal
Guitar I
Guitar II
Bass
Drums
D
G
F

Em
D
G
Vocal
Guitar I
Guitar II
Bass
Drums
F
Em
E G5
A5
B5
A5
Now the world is

G5 F#5 B5 A5 B5 C#5 B5 A5 B5 C#5 G5 A5 B5 A5
Vocal
gone, I'm just one. Oh God, help me. Hold my breath as
Guitar I
Guitar II
Bass
Drums
G5 F#5 B5 A5 B5 C#5 B5 A5 B5 C#5 G5 A5 B5 A5 G5 F#5 B5
I wish for death. Oh please God, help me!
M

F
Am
G
B5
C
Am
G
Vocal
Guitar I
Guitar II
Bass
Drums
( ) = (Another Gt.)
g
M
(M)

B
C
Am
G
B5
C
Vocal
Guitar I
Guitar II
Bass
Drums

Am
G
B
Vocal
Guitar I
Guitar II
Bass
Drums
C
G
Em
D
B5
M
g
T
A
B

C5
Em
D
B5
Vocal
Guitar I
Guitar II
Bass
Drums
M
g
C5
Em

H
E5
Vocal
Guitar I
Guitar II
Bass
Drums
E5
F5
E5
F5
E5
F5

E5
F5
E5
F5
I
E5
Vocal
Dark - ness im - pris - on - ing me,
Land - mine has tak - en my sight,
Guitar I
M
Guitar II
Bass
Drums
E5
F5
E5
1.
F5
all that I see, ab - so - lute hor - ror! I can - not live! I can - not die! Trapped in my - self, bod - y, my hold - ing
tak - en my speech, tak - en my hear - ing, tak - en my arms, tak - en my legs,

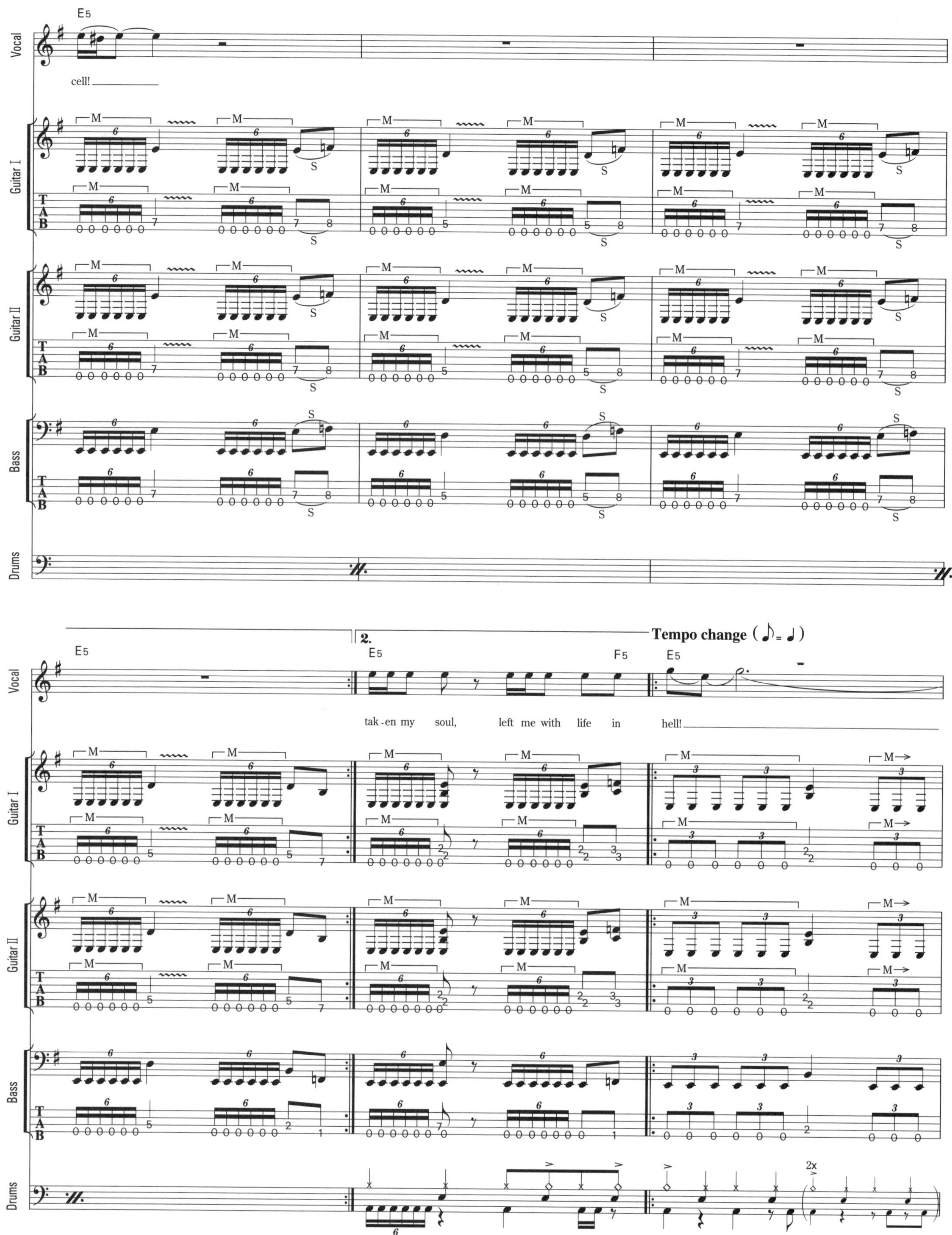
E5
Vocal
cell!
Guitar I
Guitar II
Bass
Drums
2.
Tempo change
F5
tak-en my soul, left me with life in hell!
2x

E5
F5
E5
F5
E5
Vocal
(M)
M
Guitar I
Guitar II
Bass
Drums
E5
F5
E5
F5
2x

E5
Vocal
Guitar I
Guitar II
Bass
Drums
J
F5
8va
M
(M)
P
H

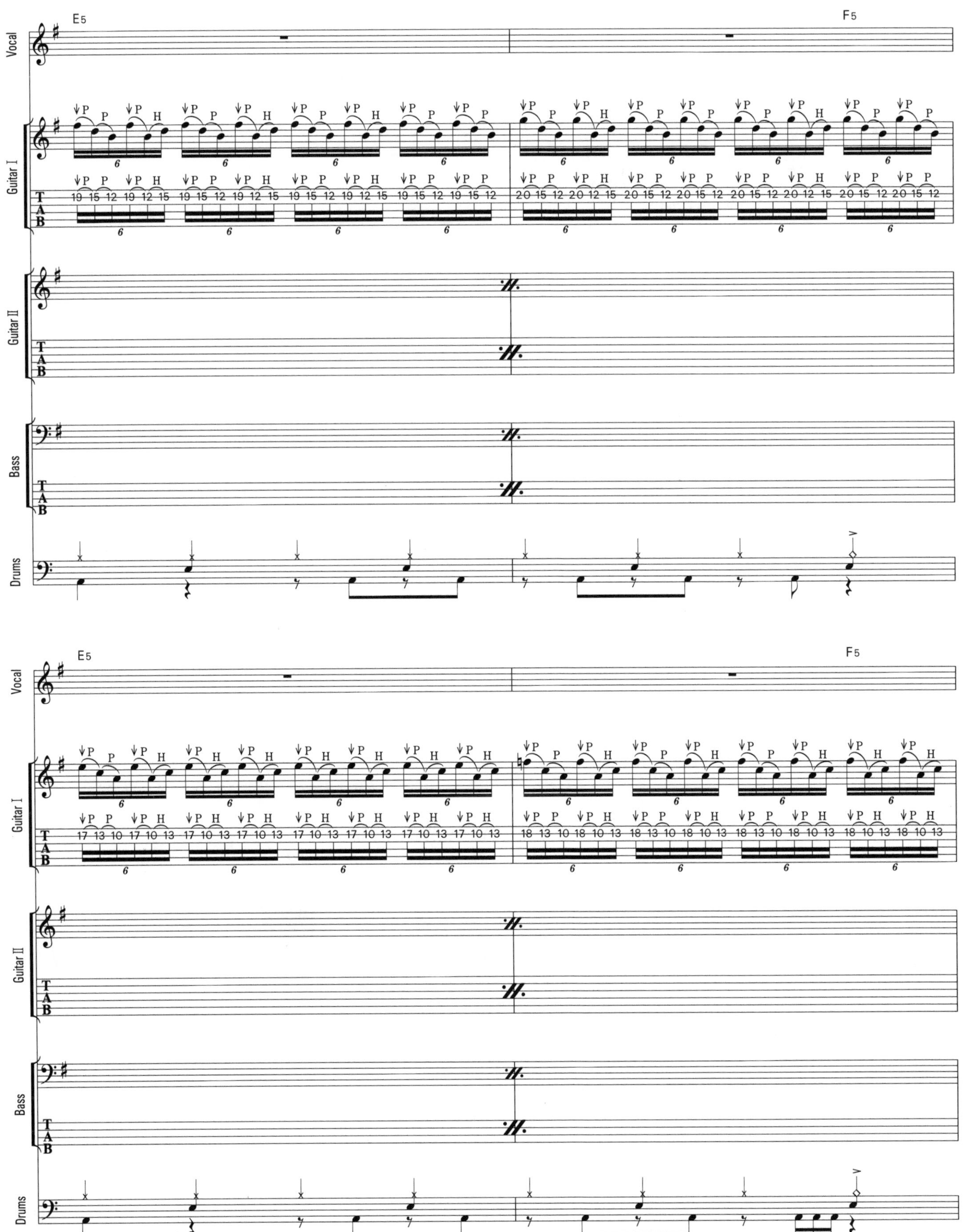
E5
F5
Vocal
Guitar I
Guitar II
Bass
Drums
E5
F5
Vocal
Guitar I
Guitar II
Bass
Drums

E5
F5
E5
Vocal
Guitar I
Guitar II
Bass
Drums
K
E5
F5
G5

E5
F5
G5
L
G5
Vocal
Guitar I
Guitar II
Bass
Drums
P
H
C
H.C
M
T
A
B

G5
A♭5
F5
G5
Vocal
Guitar I
Guitar II
Bass
Drums
M

G5
F5
Vocal
Guitar I
8va
H.C
D
P
C
Guitar II
M
Bass
Drums

G5
N
E5
F5
Vocal
Guitar I
Guitar II
Bass
Drums
M
T
A
B
E5
F5
E5
F5

E5
F5
E5
Vocal
Guitar I
Guitar II
Bass
Drums
M
H.C
C
D
O
2x

E5
F5
E5
F5
Vocal
Guitar I
Guitar II
Bass
Drums
H.C
C
D
2x
1.
2.
(M)
M

E5
F5
P
E5
Vocal
Guitar I
Guitar II
Bass
Drums
M
(M)
E5
F5
E5
F5
E5

E5
F5
Q
E5
F5
Vocal
Guitar I
Guitar II
Bass
Drums
M
2x
G5
R
E5
F5

1.
2.
E5
F5
G5
Vocal
Guitar I
Guitar II
Bass
Drums
M
S
E5
F5
E5

Until It Sleeps

Words and Music by James Hetfield and Lars Ulrich

A
Am
Vocal
Where do I take this pain of mine?
Guitar I
Guitar II
Bass
Drums
Am
I run but it stays right by my side.

B
Am G F Am G F
Vocal
So tear me o - pen, pour me out, there's things in side that scream and shout.
Guitar I
Guitar II
Bass
Drums
Am G F Am G Fmaj7
And the pain still hates me, so hold me un til it sleeps.

C
Am
Vocal
Guitar I
Guitar II
Bass
Drums
D
Am
Just like the curse, just like the stray.
Arm
Arm

Am
Vocal
You feed it once and now it stays, now it stays.
Guitar I
Guitar II
Bass
S
Drums
E
Am G F Am G F
1. So tear me o - pen but be - ware, there's things in - side with - out a care.
2. I'll tear me o - pen make you gone. No more can you hurt an - y - one.
M
H
g
P P S

Am
G
F
Am
G
Vocal
And the dirt still stains me,
And the fear still shakes me,
so wash me
so hold me
Guitar I
Guitar II
Bass
Drums
2x
G
F
F
Em
un - til I'm clean.
un - til it sleeps.
It grips you, so hold me.

Em
Vocal
It stains you, so hold me.
Guitar I
Guitar II
Bass
Drums
Em
It hates you, so hold me.
2x

Em
1.
It holds you, so hold me
Vocal
Guitar I
Guitar II
Bass
Drums
G
Am
Un - til it sleeps. Un - til it sleeps.
un - til it sleeps.

Am
H Am
Vocal
So tell me why you've cho - sen me.
Guitar I
Guitar II
Arm
Arm
Bass
S
g
Drums
6
Am
Don't want your grip, don't want your greed.

Am
2.
Em
Vocal
Don't want it.
It holds you, holds you, holds you,
Guitar I
Guitar II
Bass
Drums
Em
I
Am
Un - til it sleeps, un - til it sleeps.
un - til it sleeps,
8va

Am
un til it sleeps, un til it sleeps.
Vocal
Guitar I
Guitar II
Bass
Drums
Am
J
C2

C2
Vocal
Don't want it.
I don't want it, want it, want it, want
Guitar I
Guitar II
Bass
Drums
Am
it, want it, no.
K
Am
G
F
So tear me o - pen but be - ware,

Am
G
F
Am
G
Vocal
there's things in - side with - out a care.
And the dirt
still stains me,
so wash me
till I'm clean.
Fmaj7
Guitar I
Guitar II
Bass
Drums

A5
D5(onA)
F(onA)
Vocal
I'll tear me o - pen make you gone.
No long - er will you hurt an - y - one.
Guitar I
Guitar II
Bass
Drums
And the hate still shapes me,
so hold me
un - til it sleeps,
H

L Am
un - til it sleeps, un - til it sleeps. un - til it sleeps, un - til it sleeps.
Vocal
Guitar I
Guitar II
Arm
Bass
S
g
Drums
M Am
rit.

Whiplash

Words and Music by James Hetfield and Lars Ulrich

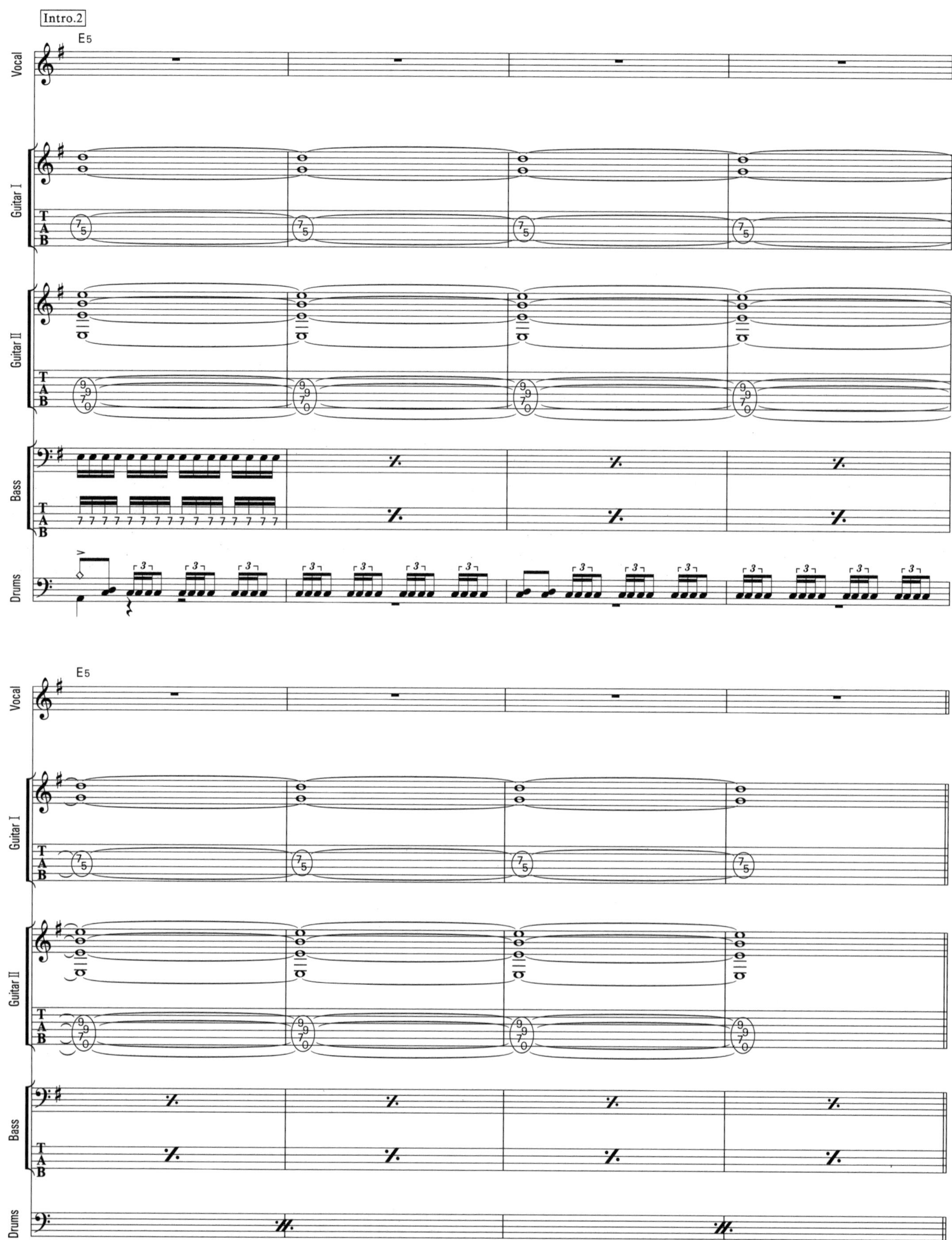
Intro.2
E5
Vocal
Guitar I
Guitar II
Bass
Drums
E5
Vocal
Guitar I
Guitar II
Bass
Drums

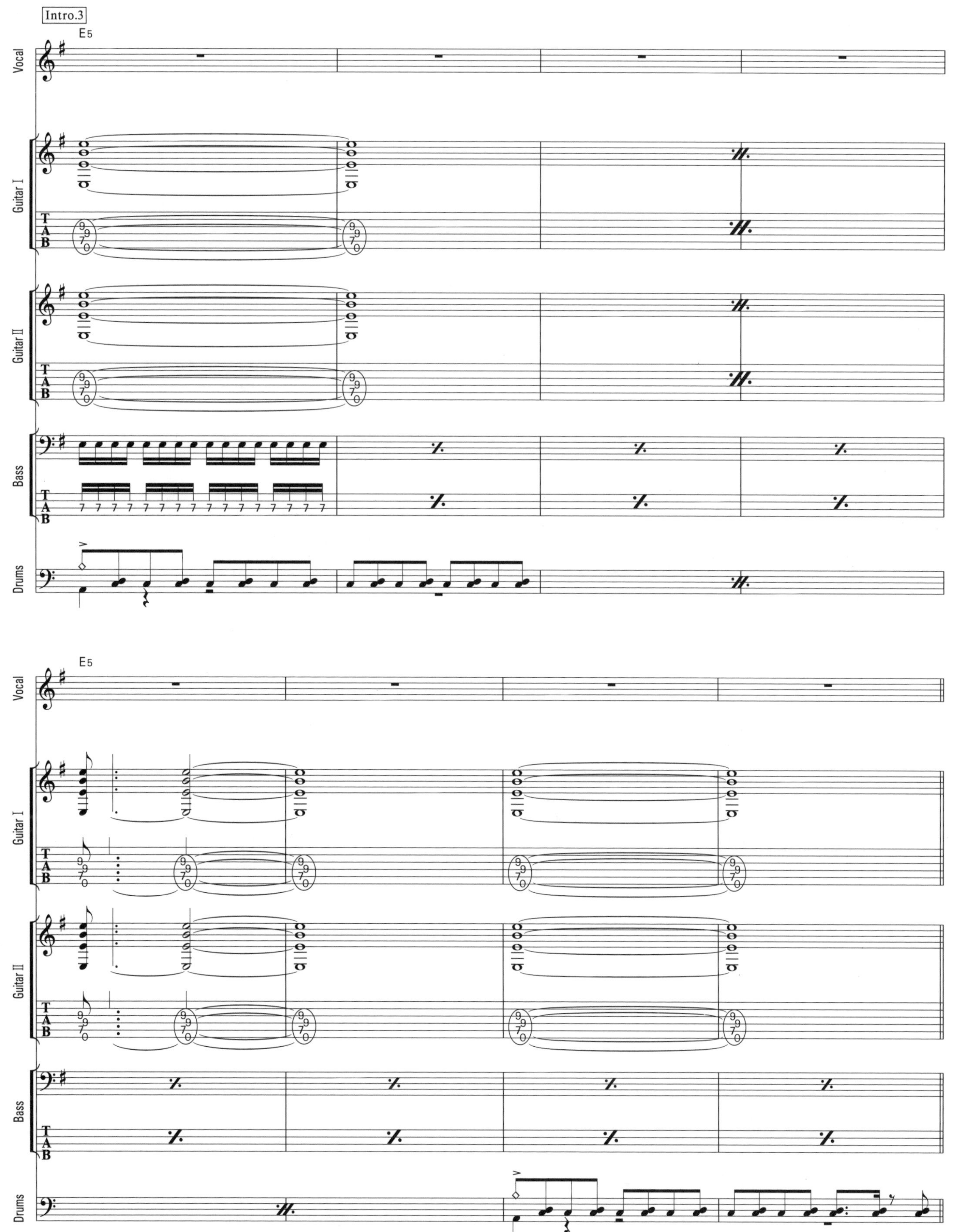
Intro.3
E5
Vocal
Guitar I
Guitar II
Bass
Drums
E5
Vocal
Guitar I
Guitar II
Bass
Drums

Intro.4
E5
A5
A♭5
1.
E5
Vocal
Guitar I
M
P
Guitar II
Bass
Drums
2x
2.
G5

Intro.5
E5
A5
A♭5
G5
E5
Vocal
Guitar I
Guitar II
Bass
Drums
M
Intro.6
E5
A5
A♭5
G5
E5
G5
2x

E5
G5
E5
G5
Vocal
Guitar I
T
A
B
Guitar II
T
A
B
Bass
T
A
B
Drums
3
E5
G5
A
E5
1. Late at night, all sys - tems go, You've
2. Bang your head a - gainst the stage like you
M
0

E5 G5 E5 G5
Vocal
come to see— the show. We do our best,— you're the rest,— you make it real you know.
nev - er did— be - fore.— Make it ring,— make it bleed— make it real - ly sore.
Guitar I
(M)
T A B
Guitar II
(M)
T A B
Bass
T A B
Drums
E5 G5 E5
Vocal
There's a feel - ing deep in - side— that drives you fuck - in' mad. A feel - ing of— a ham - mer head,— you
In a fren - zied mad - ness with your lea - thers and— your spikes, heads are bobb - ing a-round,— it's
Guitar I
T A B
Guitar II
T A B
Bass
T A B
Drums

E5
G5
B
C5
B5
A5
F♯5
E5
Vocal
need it oh so bad.
hot as hell to - night.
A - dren - a - line starts to flow.
Guitar I
Guitar II
Bass
Drums
M
H
2x
C5
B5
A5
F♯5
E5
C5
B5
A5
You're thrash - ing all a - round.

F♯5
E5
N.C.
C
E5
Vocal
Act - ing like a ma - ni - ac.
Whip - lash!
Guitar I
Guitar II
Bass
Drums
M
(M)
E5
A5
A♭5
G5

E5
A5
A♭5
G5
E5
Vocal
Guitar I
Guitar II
Bass
Drums
E5
A5
A♭5
G5
D
E5
G5
3. Here on stage the Mar - shall noise is pierc - ing through your ears. It
4. (The) show is through the met - al is gone, it's time to hit the road. An -
M
2x
C
(8va)
(M)

E5
G5
E5
Vocal
kicks your ass, kicks your face, ex - plod - ing feel - ing nears.
- oth - er town, an - oth - er gig, a - gain we will ex - plode.
Now's the time to let it rip, to
Ho - tel rooms and mo - tor - ways,
Guitar I
M
T
A
B
Guitar II
Bass
Drums
E5
G5
E5
G5
let it fuck - in' loose.
life out here is raw.
We're gath - ered here to maim and kill 'cause this is what we choose.
But we'll nev - er stop, we'll nev - er quit 'cause we're Met - al - li - ca.

E
C5
B5
A5
F♯5
E5
Vocal
A - dren - a - line starts to flow.
You're
thrash - ing all a - round.
Act - ing like a ma - ni - ac.
to Φ
Guitar I
Guitar II
Bass
Drums
T
A
B
M
H

N.C.
D5 D♭5 C5 A5 A♭5 G5
Vocal
Guitar I
Guitar II
Bass
Drums
F Em7
M
P
2x

1.
2.
Em7
Em7
G Em7
Vocal
Here we go!
Guitar I
Guitar II
Bass
Drums
Em7

Em7
Vocal
Guitar I
8va
Guitar II
Bass
Drums
Em7
Vocal
Guitar I
Guitar II
Bass
Drums

Em7
Vocal
Guitar I
Guitar II
Bass
Drums
Em7
Vocal
Guitar I
Guitar II
Bass
Drums

Vocal
Guitar I
Guitar II
Bass
Drums
E5
Whip - lash!
H
A5
A♭5
G5

E5
A5
A♭5
G5
Vocal
Guitar I
Guitar II
Bass
Drums
8va
D.S.

Coda
C5
B5
A5
I
E5
F#5
E5
F#5
E5
F#5
E5
F#5
E5
F#5
E5
F#5
E5
E5
F#
E5
F#5
E5
F#5
E5
F#5
Wo oh!
Vocal
Guitar I
Guitar II
Bass
Drums

NOTATION LEGEND

The music in this book is transcribed with the utmost attention to detail. However, it is recommended that you listen to the recording and pay close attention to subtle nuances and untranscribable rhythm of the music.

Please note that the music for each part is transcribed in a different format. For instance, for the male vocal, guitar and bass guitar parts, the music is noted an octave higher than the actual sounding pitch. The music for a keyboard instrument such as the piano is noted at actual pitch. Please keep the foregoing in mind when playing the keyboard part using a guitar.

Now we would like to explain the notation in this book for the guitar, the bass guitar and the drum parts respectively.

GUITAR

The following are the explanations for each symbol:

1) C : Bend
- C → Bend (whole step)
- HC → Bend (half step)
- 1HC → Bend (whole and half steps)
- 2C → Bend (two whole steps)
- QC → Slight Bend (microtone)

Letters or numbers printed before the C represent how high a note is to be bent.

2) U : Prebend (string bent before picking)
The U is considered different from C as the string is bent before picking.

3) D : Release
Release the bent string to its normal pitch. This D is equivalent to the latter half of Bend (or Prebend) and Release.

4) H : Hammer-On

5) P : Pull-Off

6) S : Legato Slide

7) tr : Trill (a combination of a fast Hammer-On/Pull-Off)

*Even if any of the above specified notes are combined with slurs, only the first note is to be struck.

8) gliss : Glissando
The Glissando is similar to the Legato Slide (S), however it does not designate exactly where the slide starts or where it ends. Since Glissando occur frequently, in some areas the note "gliss" may be omitted. Instead, slanted lines are used to express ascending and descending.

9) ~~~ : Vibrato

10) Harm : Natural Harmonic

11) (Ph): Pinch Harmonic
Add the edge of the thumb or the tip of the index finger of the pick hand to the normal pick attack.

12) ↓ : Tapping
Hammer the fret indicated with the pick hand finger.

13) ×(with stem) : There are three meanings to this note.
1. A vague note which its actual pitch cannot be recognized.
2. A note impossible to tell its pitch (rare).
3. Fret-Hand muting with the left hand in a chord form (percussive tone).

BASS GUITAR

The notes are in bass clef (F clef). Some symbols for the bass are similar to those of the guitar, so it would be necessary for you to learn the above-mentioned guitar notations before you play.

DRUMS

From the space above the top line of the stave; G:Tom-tom, E:Snare drum, C:Bass tom-tom, A:Kick drum, ◇ on higher B:cymbal, × on higher B:high hat (o → open, × → close), × on lower F:high-hat (hit by pressing the pedal)